AF480933

My twin and I may look the same,
but we are different in many ways.

He is silly, and I am serious.

He likes vegetables that I think are yucky!

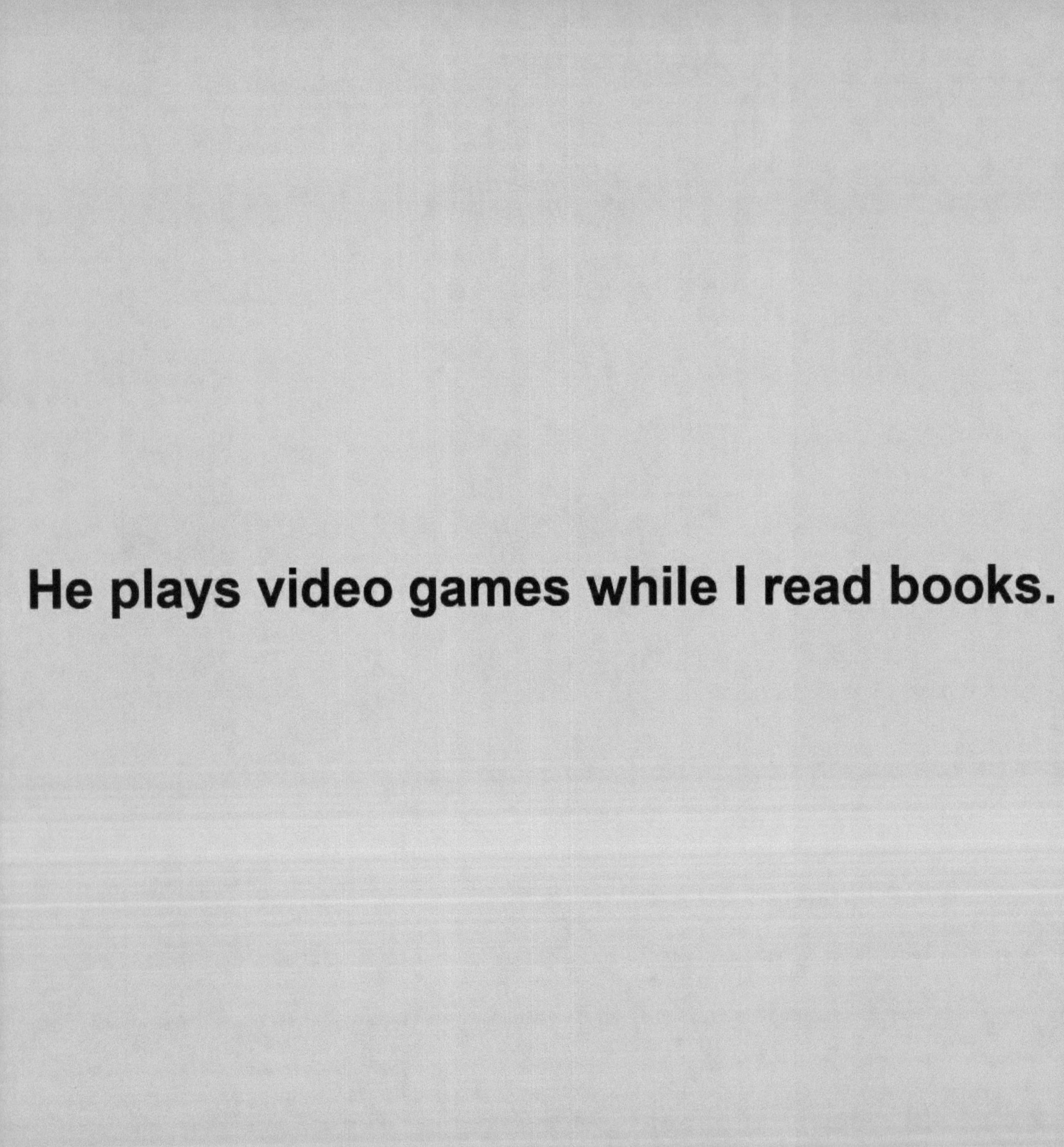

He plays video games while I read books.

He makes messes,
but I help Mommy clean them up.

HELLO

He is adventurous,
and I am very cautious.

He is big, but I am small.

He knows how to tie
his shoes, but I do not.

He cannot spell his name, but I sure can!

He likes cars, but I prefer dinosaurs.

He likes to swing, and I like to slide.

He likes dogs, but I like cats.

We may be different,
but we love each other the same!